ISBN 978-1-5284-5789-7
PIBN 10937314

# 1 MONTH OF
# FREE
# READING

## at

## www.ForgottenBooks.com

By purchasing this book you are
eligible for one month membership to
ForgottenBooks.com, giving you
unlimited access to our entire
collection of over 1,000,000 titles via
our web site and mobile apps.

To claim your free month visit:

www.forgottenbooks.com/free937314

**English**
**Français**
**Deutsche**
**Italiano**
**Español**
**Português**

# www.forgottenbooks.com

**Mythology** Photography **Fiction**
Fishing Christianity **Art** Cooking
Essays Buddhism Freemasonry
Medicine **Biology** Music **Ancient**
**Egypt** Evolution Carpentry Physics
Dance Geology **Mathematics** Fitness
Shakespeare **Folklore** Yoga Marketing
**Confidence** Immortality Biographies
Poetry **Psychology** Witchcraft
Electronics Chemistry History **Law**
Accounting **Philosophy** Anthropology
Alchemy Drama Quantum Mechanics
Atheism Sexual Health **Ancient History**
**Entrepreneurship** Languages Sport
Paleontology Needlework Islam
**Metaphysics** Investment Archaeology
Parenting Statistics Criminology
**Motivational**

imph.
HMod.
W.

# War and
# The Workers

A Study Guide for the use of Study Circles,
Classes, and Individual Students on questions
arising out of the Great European War.

Published by
*The Workers' Educational Association,*
*14, Red Lion Square, London, W.C.*
1915

# Introduction.

THIS Guide to Study is issued in answer to the large demand which has arisen all over the country for help in studying the causes that have led our civilisation to the catastrophe which has befallen it. The Yorkshire District of the W.E.A. brought out an excellent Guide to Study as a supplement to the September number of *The Highway*; this has been very widely used, and with admirable result. But there are now very many who desire to approach the subject from different points of view, and to work out thoroughly some one aspect of it ; their aim is not so much to get a first understanding of the general situation, but rather to pursue as effectively as possible some one of the lines of enquiry opened up by this war. It is for these that the Guide now issued is designed.

The aim has been to be as thorough and yet as concise as possible. Of course it is not for a moment contemplated that any group of working men will attempt all the courses here sketched out. Such an attempt would require the lifetime of a professional student. But previous interest or study has made different groups or individuals eager to raise and try to answer certain questions, and we hope that any such may find in this little book suggestions as to how he may set about solving the problem which he desires to raise. We have only considered serious students who are ready to take time and trouble. Almost any one of the sections outlined is enough for a three years' course. For, after all, what the war has brought home to us is not so much our need of knowledge in order that we may contribute to a sound public opinion on the crisis, but rather the vital importance of entire fields of study which hitherto have been to a large extent neglected.

I have spoken of " our " aim ; but must say in honesty that none of the credit for the labour represented by this book belongs to me ; but I am glad, as President of the W.E.A., to introduce to our members the product of much W.E.A. experience and toil.

W. TEMPLE.

# WAR AND THE WORKERS.

## WHAT A STUDY CIRCLE IS.

A Study Circle is a group of people who meet regularly to help one another to a knowledge of some subject. The number of members may be as small as three, but there should not be more than twenty to twenty-four, or free discussion will become difficult.

## HOW TO FORM A STUDY CIRCLE.

A meeting should be called of those who wish to join a Circle, and at this meeting should be decided the time and place of the regular meetings of the Circle, and also the subject to be studied. It is desirable, too, that a Secretary should be elected.

Meetings should not be infrequent. Weekly meetings are preferable, and if they are held at a greater interval than a fortnight there is a danger of members losing interest.

The meetings may be held anywhere, but a social club is better than a class room, and a room in a private house better than a club.

## PROCEDURE.

There are several methods of conducting a Study Circle, and the members must decide which method is best suited to their needs.

(1) A regular leader may be appointed, whose duty it would be to open each evening with a brief " talk " on the subject selected. He would also act as chairman in the subsequent discussion.

(2) The leader may only be called upon to act as chairman and the paper of the evening may be contributed by the members in turn.

(3) A leader may be dispensed with altogether and the member who contributes the paper would in this case act as chairman for the evening.

At the preliminary meeting, at which the subject is decided, it will be found advisable to divide the subject into sections and to allocate a section to each evening, and, in the case of the adoption of either (2) or (3), the members to be responsible for the papers should also be selected.

## BOOKS.

In many cases reference has been made to a number of books, since it is probable that only one or two will be within reach; but at the same time an attempt has been made to make the fullest possible use of a few good, and fairly cheap, books.

*All the book prices quoted are net.*

The W.E.A. Book Department (Central Office, 14, Red Lion Square, London, W.C.) will be glad to deal with any book orders.

The W.E.A. Central Library (Toynbee Hall, Commercial Street, London, E.) will welcome any enquiries as to further books on any subject dealt with in this booklet, and will gladly help any Class, Study Circle, or Individual Student as far as possible.

Immediately a subject is selected the Secretary of the Circle should make out a list of the books recommended in the Study Guide and ascertain how many of them are in the local Public Library; he should then supply the information to the members, and should also take steps to see that the Library Committee is asked to add the books that are not in.

The following books are not mentioned in the Study Guide, but they should be in every good Reference Library and should be referred to throughout :—

"Encyclopædia Britannica." For concise, reliable accounts of all statesmen, treaties, countries, wars, etc.

"Cambridge Modern History" (Vols. X., XI., XII.). For the policy and internal history of different countries.

"Statesman's Year Book." For exact details of constitution, population, resources, etc., of different countries.

"Geography of Europe," Lyde.

"Everyman Atlas." Four vols. 1/- each.

Students will find it useful to read the articles by Hilaire Belloc in "Land and Water" (6d. weekly).

## I.—CAUSES OF THE WAR.

### (a) FACTS RELATING TO THE ACTUAL OUTBREAK OF WAR.

A study of the causes of the war should commence with an enquiry concerning the events immediately preceding the outbreak, and especially the events from July 25th to August 4th.

BOOKS : "The Diplomatic History of the War," by M. P. Price (7/6), contains all published diplomatic documents issued by the various nations, except the French Yellow Book (Foreign Office, 1d.), and also contains reports of debates in various European Parliaments at outbreak of war.
"Great Britain and the European Crisis" (Government Blue Book, 1d.) presents the situation from the British side.
The case for Britain is also presented in "Why we are at War" (2/- and 2/6), which contains an English translation of the German White Paper, and copies of the original notes and

telegrams; "Why Britain is at War" and "How Britain strove for Peace" (pamphlets by Sir E. Cook, 2d.), and in the September Number of "The Round Table" (of which copies may still be obtained by W.E.A. members and students for 1/2 post free).

Writings from the German point of view are not easily obtainable in this country, but a German book entitled "The Truth about Germany," purporting to give the German side of the case, has been published in English and distributed in America. It has been reprinted in England by Douglas Sladen, under the title of "Germany's Great Lie" (1/-). Unfortunately, the comments of Mr. Sladen are interspersed through the book, breaking the sequence of the German argument and detracting from its value.

## (b) HISTORICAL CAUSES.

### 1. *The History of Europe*, 1814 *to* 1870.

Study the character of the Congress of Vienna, and compare the professions of disinterestedness with the similar professions current at the present time. The ideas of the leading representatives (*i.e.*, Metternich, Alexander, Talleyrand, Castlereagh, etc.) should also be carefully studied. Note the main lines of the resettlement of Europe laid down in the Treaty and also its defects, as seen in subsequent history. Endeavour to trace the defects to their sources. Study the character and aims of (1) The European Concert; (2) The Holy Alliance. Note their respective attitudes toward the growth of liberal ideas and institutions.

BOOKS: Levett: "Europe since Napoleon" (2/8), intro. and ch. i gives a clear, tabulated statement of the main provisions of the Treaty and also its effect upon the relative positions of the chief countries of Europe. The chief Congresses of the European Concert, from 1815 to 1822 are also summarised. See also Alison Phillips: "Modern Europe" (6/-), intro., Perris: "History of War and Peace' (Home University Library, 1/-), chap. x; and Hawkesworth: "The Last Century in Europe" (5/-).

A criticism of the Congress of Vienna from the standpoint of nationality will be found in "War and Democracy," ch. ii, sec. 3.

### 2. *Europe since* 1870.

The period from 1870 to the present day may be called the period of "Armed Peace." Study the causes which led to the decay of the European Concert and the substituting of "alliances."

BOOKS: Alison Phillips: "Modern Europe," chs. xix and xx. Gooch: "History of Our Time" (1/-). Holland Rose: "Development of European Nations since 1870" (7/6). The following Oxford pamphlets will be found useful :— "French Policy since 1871," F. Morgan and H. W. C. Davis (2d.) "Austrian Policy since 1867," Murray Beaven (3d.). "Italian Policy since 1870," Keith Feiling (2d.). See also general Histories, such as Seignobos: "Political History of Contemporary Europe" (2 vols., 10/-), and Andrews: "The Historical Development of Modern Europe" (12/6).

## (c) Underlying Causes.

### 1. *The National Idea,* 1789-1914.

Note the influences of (i) the partition of Poland, and (ii) the French Revolution and conquests in arousing and spreading the national idea in Europe. Trace this idea in the chief European wars of the 19th and 20th centuries.

> Books : " War and Democracy," ch. ii gives an excellent account of the development of the national idea and contrasts the working out of the idea in German unity and in Italian unity. See also " Essays of Mazzini " (Everyman, 1/-).
> In " Lectures on the History of the 19th Century," edited by Kirkpatrick (Cambridge Univ. Press, 4/6), lecture ii, will be found a general survey of international history during the century.
> For the working out of the national idea in the different countries see " Lectures on History of the 19th Century," lectures x and xi (for Italy), lectures v and vi (for Germany ; Alison Phillips : " Modern Europe," chs. iii and xvi (for Germany), ch. xv (for Italy), ch. vii (for Greece); also histories of the various countries.
> The following Oxford Pamphlets will be found useful :—
> " The National Principle and the War," Ramsay Muir (3d).
> " Serbia and the Serbs," Sir Valentine Chirol (2d.).
> " The Eastern Question," F. F. Urquhart (3d.).

### 2. *The struggle for hegemony in Europe.*

(i) Trace the successive efforts of Continental powers to dominate Europe from the 16th century to the present day. Note the attempts of Charles V., Louis XIV, Napoleon I, and, in a lesser degree, Napoleon III. (See also Section on Foreign Policy.)

It will perhaps be found advisable to confine attention to one only of these monarchs : in this case the career of Napoleon I should be studied.

> Books : Details of the various attempts at European hegemony and the steps taken to defeat them will be found in Burrows : " History of Foreign Policy of Great Britain " (6/-). See also Magnus : " Third Great War " (1/-).
> General histories of Europe should be consulted, and also the biographies of the monarchs. The following books on Napoleon will be found useful :—
> Fisher : " Napoleon " (Home University Library, 1/-)
> Johnston : " Napoleon " (4/6).
> Seeley : " Life of Napoleon " (3/9).
> On the question of hegemony see Cramb : " Germany and England " (2/6), pp. 108-121.

(ii) Study the efforts to secure supremacy for races and cultures, as seen in the Pan-German and the Pan-Sclavonic movements. Is there a Pan-British movement ? Consider how far the Pan-German movement is justified by the policy of England as seen in Colonial Expansion, Sea Power, Imperialism, etc. Note the effects of these movements in provoking mutual fear and strained relations.

Books : Much more accurate information is available concerning the Pan-German movement than other movements since it has been more carefully and openly organised. For accounts of it see von Bülow : " Imperial Germany " (2/-), ch. 1 ; Bernhardi : " Germany and the Next War " (2/-), particularly chs. iii, iv, and v. A criticism of the movement will be found in Usher's " Pan-Germanism " (2/-), but students should also read Bourdon's " The German Enigma " (2/6).
In Cramb : " Germany and England," lecture i, secs. ii-v, will be found a discussion of Pan-Germanism particularly in relation to England. This aspect may also be studied in Sarolea : " The Anglo-German Problem " (2./-), chs. ix, xi, xiii, and xiv.
See also Brailsford : " Origins of the Great War " ; and Russell : " War, the Offspring of Fear " (Pamphlets of the Union of Democratic Control, 1d.).
On the question of British Imperialism see Sir Chas. Lucas' " Greater Rome and Greater Britain."

### 3. *The struggle for economic advantage.*

Note the efforts of Great Powers to secure political control of backward countries in order (1) to add the mineral wealth of such countries to their resources ; (2) to win for their own subjects opportunities of commercial and financial exploitation. In the case of Germany, how far is her policy due to her need to keep open some markets (*e.g.*, Morocco) or her desire to monopolise others (*e.g.*, Mesopotamia) for her people ?

How far is the influence of finance thrown on the side of peace ?

Books : H. N. Brailsford : " War of Steel and Gold " (5/-), and Norman Angell : " Foundations of International Polity " (3/6), especially chap. iii.

### (d) Philosophical Causes.

This section should not be attempted unless the help of a competent leader is available.

The influence of ideas may be more clearly traced in the present war than in any previous war. These ideas fall into two groups, (1) the " ends " of national policy, and (2) the " means " which may legitimately be adopted. For the sake of clearness the two should be studied separately.

### 1. *The " ends " of national policy.*

(i) Note how the materialism of the 18th century was challenged by Kant, who, in the place of " force," put " law " and the idea of unity, connection and organisation. Trace the development of this Idealism through Fichte and Hegel and the conception by the latter of the State as the embodiment of freedom. Note also how Idealism came to dominate the English Universities and to modify the English national outlook.

(ii) Trace the reaction against Idealism through Schopenhauer, Feuerbach, Büchner (" Force and Matter "), Haeckel (" Riddle of the Universe "), and Nietzsche (" The Will to Power ").

(iii) Note the way in which German historians and politicians have applied the reactionary ideas to justify German aspirations to world power.

Books: (i) Kant: "The Theory of Ethics," tr. by Abbott (Longman, 12/6).
" Essay on Perpetual Peace " (Sonnenschein, 2/-).
*Commentary* : Wallace's " Kant" (Blackwood, 1/-).
Fichte: " Science of Rights (9/6), " introduction and second appendix.
" The Nature of the Scholar," introduction, tr. by Smith. In Popular Works, 2 vols. (21/-).
*Commentary* : Adamson's " Fichte" (1/-).
Hegel : " Philosophy of Right," Eng. Trns. Dyde (5/8), part iii, sec. iii.
*Commentary* : Caird's " Hegel" (1/-).
(ii) Schopenhauer: "The World as Will and Idea," 3 vols. (27/-).
*Commentary* : Wallace's " Schopenhauer" (1/-).
Feuerbach : " Essence of Christianity" (K. Paul, o.p.).
Max Stirner : " The Ego and His Own " (2/6).
Buchner : " Force and Matter" (Asher, o.p.).
Haeckel : " Riddle of the Universe" (Watts, 6d.), ch. xiv
Nietzsche : "Beyond Good and Evil" (2/6).
" The Will to Power " (1/-).
*Commentary* : Mügge's " Friedrich Nietzsche " (6d.).
(iii) Treitschke : Gowan : "Selections from the Treitschke's Lectures on Politics " (2/-).
Hausrath : " Treitschke, His Life and Works " (7/6).
H. C. W. Davis : " Political Thoughts of Heinrich von Treitschke " (6/-).
Barker : " Nietzsche and Treitschke " (Oxford Pamphlets, 2d.).
Bernhardi : " Germany and the Next War " (2/-), chs. i, ii, and iv.
The following should also be consulted :—
Külpe : " The Philosophy of the Present in Germany " (Allen, 3/6).
Lange : " History of Materialism," vol. ii, bk. ii, ch. ii. (3/-).
*Note* :—Students will probably find that the books under the heading of " Commentary " are most helpful, especially if the time for reading is limited.

## 2. *Disregard for law.*

It is advisable to examine very carefully the German Chancellor's statement. " Necessity knows no law." Leaving out of account for the time being the exigencies of the German position, discuss (i) to what extent disregard for law, agreements and promises is justifiable, and (ii) the growth of this disregard during the last ten years. Consider the claim that the teachings of Bergson may be held to justify this disregard. Should law and agreements be regarded as inviolable under all circumstances ? How do we regard the defiance of law or breach of agreement in our own social, political, and industrial life ?

Books : Bernhardi : " Germany and the Next War."
" Selections from Treitschke," bk. i, sec. iii.
Cole : " World of Labour " (5/-), ch. ix (see also index).
Carr : " Henri Bergson " (People's Books, 6d.).
Harley : " Syndicalism " (People's Books, 6d.)
Macdonald : " Syndicalism " (1/-).
Thoreau : " Duty of Civil Disobedience " (3d.).

## II.—THE ECONOMIC ASPECT OF THE WAR.

### (a) FOREIGN COMMERCE.

The present war differs from previous wars not only in the scale of its operations, but also in its far-reaching effects upon nations other than belligerents : discuss the reason for this.

Study how debts between nations are paid ; the importance of credit ; also what a moratorium is and why it was declared.

Note that Great Britain has based its economic activities on the assumption of continued peace, while Germany has based hers on the possibility of war. Study the steps taken by Germany.

> BOOKS : " War and Democracy," ch. viii, for the discussion of the whole question ; also " Lombard Street in War " (September number of " The Round Table ") and " The War and Financial Exhaustion " (in the December number) ; Brailsford : " War of Steel and Gold " (5 /-) ; and Ashley : " The War in its Economic Aspect " (Oxford Pamphlets, 2d.).
> On the question of International Exchange consult any of the following :—
> Bastable : " International Trade " (3 /6), chs. iii. iv. and v.
> Withers : " Meaning of Money " (3 /-).
> Barker : " Cash and Credit " (Cambridge Manuals, 1 /-).
> Clare : " A B.C. of Foreign Exchanges " (3 /-).
> For particulars of Germany's commercial preparations see Bernhardi : " Germany and the Next War," ch. xiv, also pp. 157-159 ; von Bulow : " Imperial Germany," pp. 220-223.
> For a discussion upon the general economic effects of war read Norman Angell : " Great Illusion " (2 /6), part i.

### (b) INDUSTRY AND INDUSTRIAL ORGANISATIONS.

Note the effects of the war upon the volume of employment, the nature of the employment (some industries are abnormally busy as the result of the war), and upon the Co-operative and Trade Union movements ; also the effect of the withdrawal from productive employment of large bodies of men (*i.e.*, by enlistment, calling up of reserves, etc.).

> BOOKS : " War and Democracy," ch. viii.
> See also the " Board of Trade Labour Gazette," 1d. monthly.

### (c) STATE ACTION.

The entry of the State into the realms of finance and industry should be discussed (*i.e.*, note the moratorium, issue of State notes, guarantee of bills, Government subsidy of marine insurance, State purchase of sugar, etc.). Discuss also State efforts to relieve distress.

> BOOKS : " War and Democracy " ch. viii.
> For suggestions concerning remedies for distress see Webb's pamphlet, " The War and the Workers " (1d.).

### (d) VOLUNTARY ACTION.

Discuss the Relief Funds and their methods of distribution ; also the Women's Employment Fund. Ought the State to rely upon voluntary effort to supply comforts to the soldiers and sailors and to relieve distress ? Consider how far it is socially and economically advantageous for these comforts to be produced by unpaid labour, particularly of people who are ordinarily non-producers.

### (e) THE ECONOMIC POSITION AFTER THE WAR.

Consider what will be the probable state of trade and industry when peace is restored. Is it possible or desirable for England to capture Germany's trade ? Consider the probable effects upon trade and industry in the event of the final issue of the war proving unfavourable to (i) the Allies, (ii) Germany. What would be the advantage to England of an indemnity paid by Germany ? The effects of the Franco-German war upon the two nations should be studied.

> BOOKS : " War and Democracy," ch. viii.
> Norman Angell : " Great Illusion,' chs. iii, iv, v, and vi.

## III.—SOCIAL ASPECT OF WAR AND WARLIKE PREPARATION.

### (a) BIOLOGICAL AND POLITICAL CONSIDERATIONS.

Is war a political necessity on biological grounds ? Discuss the statement " War is one of the elements of order in the world, established by God." Consider the relation of the theories of biological evolution to social and political evolution. Do the principles of " the struggle for existence " and " the survival of the fittest " apply to nations ? Study war from the standpoint of Eugenics. Can one nation permanently establish its supremacy over another nation by force ? Does preparedness for war really increase national safety and prevent war ?

> BOOKS : On the application of biological laws to political evolution read Haeckel : " Riddle of the Universe," ch. xiv ; Strauss : " The Old Faith and the New" (o.p.), secs. 74-80, Eng. tr. ; Bernhardi : " Germany and the Next War," introduction and chs. i and ii. For criticism of such application of biological laws read Bagehot : " Physics and Politics " (1/-), chs. ii, iii, and iv ; Ritchie : " Darwinism and Politics " (2/6), particularly secs. 1-4; Wallas : " Great Society " (7/6), ch ix ; Hobhouse : " Democracy and Reaction " (1/-), ch. iv ; Hobhouse : " Social Evolution and Political Theory" (6/-) ; Norman Angell : " Great Illusion," part ii, chs. i-iv. For Darwin's biological ideas see Darwin : " Origin of Species " (1/-), ch. iii. Norman Angell also discusses the possibility of war promoting national greatness and power.

### (b) MORAL AND SOCIAL CONSIDERATIONS.

Consider the effect upon society and upon the character of the individual of war and warlike preparation. What is the moral effect of universal military service ? Define " militarism " and discuss its effect upon social ideas of justice and freedom. (In this connection consider the Dreyfus case and the Zabern incident.)

> BOOKS : On the moral value of war see " Selections from Treitschke."
> book iv, sec. xxiii ; Ruskin : " Crown of Wild Olive " (1/-),
> lecture iii ; " Queen of the Air " (1/-), lecture iii, secs, 114-119 ;
> Bernhardi : " Germany and the Next War," pp. 26-29.
> In criticism of the moral value of war see Wallas : "Great
> Society," ch. ix ; Angell : "Great Illusion," pp. 240-256,
> 272-283 ; Ruskin : " Sesame and Lilies," lecture i, secs 46-48 ;
> James : " Memories and Studies " (paper on " The moral
> equivalent for war ") ; Tolstoi, Works ; " Tolstoi " by Miss
> Winstanley (Jacks, 6d.) ; Wilson : " Friends and the War "
> (1d.).
> An estimation of the effect of military service upon the German
> worker may be found in Dawson : " Evolution of Modern
> Germany " (5/-), ch. ix.

## IV.—AUSTRIA-HUNGARY AND THE EASTERN QUESTION.

The student is recommended to provide himself with a Racial map. An excellent coloured map will be found (No. 7) in the " Literary and Historical Atlas of Europe " (Everyman, 1/-), and in the December number of " Round Table." Uncoloured maps are included in " War and Democracy," and also in Professor Ramsay Muir's " The National Principle and the War " (Oxford Pamphlets, 3d.).

Study (i) the part played by Austria in stemming the tide of Turkish invasion, and the interest of Austria in the future of the Balkans, (ii) the relations between Austria and Hungary, (iii) the racial question in the Dual Monarchy, (iv) the struggle of the Balkan peoples to secure national independence ; note the extent to which the present war is due to their national aspirations being baulked.

> BOOKS : For a general survey of the whole question see " War and
> Democracy," ch. iv.
> On Austria-Hungary read Levett : " Europe since Napoleon,"
> ch. vii ; " Lectures on the History of the 19th Century,"
> lecture vii ; Alison Phillips : " Modern Europe," ch. xiii ;
> Seton-Watson : " Racial Problems in Hungary" (16/-) ;
> H. W. Steed : " The Hapsburg Monarchy " (7/6).
> On the Balkans read Levett : " Europe since Napoleon,"
> ch. ix ; " History of the 19th Century," lecture xiv ; Gooch :
> " History of our Time " (Home University Library, 1/-),
> ch. v ; also Miller : " The Balkans " (3/9).
> For a statement of the Eastern Question in its relation to the
> present war see the article on " The Austro-Serbian Dispute " in
> the September number of " The Round Table."
> The following Oxford Pamphlets will be found useful :—
> " The National Principle and the War " (3d.).
> "Serbia and the Serbs " (2d.).
> " The Eastern Question " (3d.).
> " Austrian Policy since 1867 " (3d.).

# V.—THE GROWTH OF THE GERMAN EMPIRE.

## (a) The Development of Political Unity.

Study the difficulties in the way of German unity, the relative positions of Prussia and Austria after the Congress of Vienna, and the character of the German Confederation. Consider the effect of the mid-continental portion of Germany contrasted with Britain's insular isolation. Note the importance of the establishment of the Zollverein in paving the way to political unity ; also the attempts made by the Liberals to bring about national unity by political methods. Study the policy of Bismarck as seen in the Danish, Austrian, and Franco-German wars.

> Books : " War and Democracy," ch. iii.
> " Germany in the 19th Century " (2/6), lecture i.
> Holland : " Germany to the Present Day " (2/-).
> Powicke : " Bismarck " (People's Books, 6d.), chs. iii-vi.
> Alison Phillips : " Modern Europe," chs. iii, xvi-xviii.
> " History of the 19th Century," lectures v and vi.
> Lichtenberger : " Evolution of Modern Germany " (10/6).

## (b) The Working Constitution of Prussia and the German Empire.

> Books : Tower : " Germany of To-day " (Home University Library, 1/-), chs. ii-v.
> Lowell : "Governments and Parties in Continental Europe " (2 vols., 21/-), chs. v, vi, and vii.
> Levett : " Europe since Napoleon," ch. xii.

## (c) Social and Economic Progress since 1870.

Discuss the thoroughness and effectiveness of the domestic policy of Germany and the care for the welfare of the citizens.

Study the educational system and compare it with the English system.

Consider the commercial expansion of Germany and endeavour to ascertain the causes of it.

What can Britain learn from German social legislation and educational and commercial systems ?

Study the conditions of the German working classes, their wages, hours of labour, housing conditions, etc. How do they spend their leisure ? What part in the life of the German workers do such movements as Trade Unionism and Co-operation play ?

> Books : For a general description of social and economic conditions in Germany see Dawson : "Evolution of Modern Germany" (5/-), and Tower : " Germany of To-day " ; A. Ashley : " Social Policy of Bismarck (2/-) ; Ashley : " Progress of German Working Classes " (1/6).
> An excellent account of the economic development of Germany will be found in " Germany in the 19th Century," lecture iv, and in lecture v of the same book will be found an equally good account of the educational system of Germany.
> Particulars of the German Trade Schools will be found in Best and Ogden : " The Problem of the Continuation School " (King, 1/-).
> Some account of German Trade Unionism will be found in Cole : "The World of Labour," ch. vi, and also in Sombart : " Socialism and the Socialist Movement " (3/6).

## (d) POLITICAL PARTIES AND IDEALS.

Study the character of the political parties and the nature of the lines which divide them. What is their attitude towards the monarchy, the military system, and the imperial and colonial aspirations of Germany? Note the difference of outlook between the North Germans and the South Germans, and between Catholics and Protestants.

> BOOKS : Lowell : "Governments and Parties, etc.," vol. ii, ch. vii.
> Dawson : "Evolution of Modern Germany," chs. xxi-xxiii.
> Sarolea : "The Anglo-German Problem," pp. 129-155, 296-305.
> von Bulow : "Imperial Germany," pp. 133-204.

## (e) LITERARY AND INTELLECTUAL GERMANY.

An excellent survey of German intellectual and literary history will be found in "Germany in the 19th Century " (Manchester Univ., 2/6), lects. ii and iii, and a brief description of the intellectual life of Germany at the present time is included in Towers' "Germany of To-day," ch. x.

See also Robertson, "Literature of Germany " (Home University Library, 1/-).

For all sections see Price Collier, "Germany and the Germans" (2/6)

## VI.—FRANCE SINCE 1870.

Note the centralisation of France, the artificial division of administrative areas and the methods of taxation. In studying the political system consider the effect of the " groups " upon the stability of Governments. In social matters note the character of the French home life and consider its influence upon the nation. Study the effect upon economic and political progress of peasant proprietorship. What has been the effect upon the religious character of the people of the conflict between clericalism and secularism? Note the character of French amusements ; also the working class conditions. Why has Syndicalism flourished in France ?

> BOOKS : For a detailed description and criticism of French politics see Lowell : "Governments and Parties, etc.," vol i, chs. i and ii.
> A general historical account of France will be found in Levett : "Europe since Napoleon," chs. ii and iii.
> A general description of the country, institutions, and its people will be found in Thomas : "France of To-day " (Home University Library, 1/-) ; in Barker : "France of the French " (6/-) ; and in Bodley : "France " (8/-).
> The character of French working class movements is discussed in Cole : "World of Labour," chs. iii and iv ; and a clear, concise account of French Syndicalism will be found in Harley : "Syndicalism " (People's Books, 6d.).
> An excellent account of the working classes will be found in Steele : "The Working Classes in France " (1/-).

## VII.—RUSSIA.

When studying Russia it is important to study *all* aspects of the nation. Much misunderstanding has arisen in other nations because one side only (*i.e.*, the revolutionary side) has as a rule been brought under notice. Discuss representative institutions in the Mir, the Zemstvo, and the beginnings of central parliamentary government in the Duma, and the proneness to idealism shown by the Romanoffs and by the Russian people generally. The Russian lack of sympathy for subject races should be discussed, and also the character of Russian aims and policy in the Balkans. Discuss the social and domestic policy of Russia. Note the intensely religious character of the people and their aptitude for co-operation, and the remarkable strength and resource of the peasantry.

BOOKS : Baring : " The Mainsprings of Russia " (2/-), and Alexinsky : " Modern Russia " (5/-) are both excellent descriptions of Russia and her people. B. Pares : " Russia and Reform " (10/6) is excellent. Sir D. Mackenzie Wallace's " Russia " (12/6) is the standard work. More expensive books covering a similar ground are Baring : " The Russian People " (10/-) ; Williams : " Russia of the Russians " (6/-) ; and Stephen Graham : " Undiscovered Russia " (12/6). Baring : " What I saw in Russia " (1/-) gives an interesting account of Russian life. Vinogradoff : " Russia : The Psychology of a Nation " (1d.).
An account of the development of Russia in modern times will be found in Skrine : " The Expansion of Russia " (4/6). See also " History of the 19th Century," lecture xiii ; and Levett : " Europe since Napoleon," ch. viii.
All Stephen Graham's works should be read ; he gives the real psychology of the people in a most interesting way.
An appreciative description of Russia, her difficulties and her possibilities, will be found in " War and Democracy," ch. v. See also article in December number of " Round Table " on " Russia and her Ideals."

## VIII.—BELGIUM.

For the history of Belgium from its separation from Holland in 1830 read Alison Phillips, " Modern Europe," ch. ix, and Levett, " Europe since Napoleon," ch. xi.

An account of Belgium and its people will be found in Boulger, " Belgium and the Belgians " (6/-).

See also Sarolea, " How Belgium saved Europe" (Nelson, 2/-).

## IX.—ITALY.

For the history of Italy in the 19th century see Alison Phillips, " Modern Europe," ch. xv ; Levett, " Europe since Napoleon," ch. iv ; and " Lectures on the History of the 19th Century," lects. x and xi ; G. M. Trevelyan's " Garibaldi's Defence of the Roman Republic, 1848-9 " (6/6) ; " Garibaldi and the Thousand, 1860 " (7/6) ; " Garibaldi and the Making of Italy " (7/6) ; and Bolton King, " Mazzini " (4/6).

For the study of Italy as she now is read Bolton King and Okey, " Italy of To-day " (6/-).

For the constitution and political system see Lowell, " Governments and Parties, etc.," vol. i, chs. iii and iv.

## X.—TURKEY.

For the history of Turkey since the Treaty of Vienna see Alison Phillips, " Modern Europe," chs. vi, vii, x, and xix ; Levett, " Europe since Napoleon," ch. ix.

For the history of Turkey, particularly in relation to the Balkans, see Miller, " Ottoman Empire " (7/6) ; " History of the 19th Century," lect. xiv ; see also the lecture in the same volume on " Pan-Islamism " ; Eliot, " Turkey in Europe " (7/6) ; Brailsford, " Macedonia " (12/6) ; Macdonald, " Turkey and the Eastern Question " (People's Books, 6d.).

For causes of the rupture see Sir E. Cook's " Britain and Turkey " (2d.).

## XI.—MISCELLANEOUS QUESTIONS BROUGHT TO PROMINENCE BY THE WAR.

(a) FOREIGN POLICY.

1. *The British Foreign Office.*

Note (i) its organisation, and (ii) its functions.

Read " War and Democracy," ch. vi.

2. *Foreign Policy in Europe since* 1814.

(i) The causes of the various important wars during the 19th and 20th centuries should be studied, together with the congresses and treaties which ended them.

BOOKS : Burrows : " History of Foreign Policy."
Alison Phillips : " Modern Europe."
Levett : " Europe since Napoleon."

(ii) Study the aims and methods in foreign policy of such leading statesmen as Metternich, Palmerston, Disraeli, Bismarck, Cavour, Napoleon, Napoleon III, Nicholas II, Lord Salisbury, Lord Rosebery, Sir Edward Grey.

BOOKS : Books as above, together with biographies (for which see book list at the end of ch. vi, " War and Democracy ").

(iii) The position in European politics of the smaller states, such as Belgium, Holland, Denmark, Sweden, Greece, Portugal, and Switzerland should be considered, and also the expediency of maintaining neutral states.

BOOKS : " Selections from Treitschke," book i, sec. i.
Bernhardi : " Germany and the Next War," pp. 109-111.
Fisher : " Value of Small States " (Oxford Pamphlets, 2d.).

(iv) Study the ideas underlying the Concert of Europe, the Balance of Power, etc. Trace the history of the British policy of the Balance of Power from Tudor times. Note its twofold aspect (*a*) self-preservation, (*b*) acceptance of European responsibility. The following questions might profitably be discussed :—

Do the interests of England make it necessary for us to have an active continental policy ?

What responsibilities have we in continental affairs.

Is it practicable to maintain a "balance of power"; does it conduce to the peace of Europe ?

Discuss the idea of a United States of Europe.

BOOKS : Burrows : "History of Foreign Policy."
Spender : "The Foundations of British Policy" (6d.).
"War and Democracy," ch. vi.
Gooch : "History of Our Time," ch. vi. (for description of Balance of Power at the close of the 19th Century).
Bernhardi : "Germany and the Next War," ch. v. (for criticism of practicability of Balance of Power).

### 3. *Criticism of European Foreign Policy.*

Consider where lies the real responsibility for foreign policy in the chief Powers (*i.e.*, England, France, Germany, Austria, Russia, Italy). How far does the absence of adequate democratic control of foreign policy affect the possibilities of war ?

Is it possible to establish any measure of democratic control ? Consider the American Committee on Foreign Relations. Would such a Committee be practicable in England ?

BOOKS : "War and Democracy," ch. vi, and Holland Rose : "The Rise of Democracy" (2/-), ch. xv, for discussion of democratic control.
Low : "Governance of England," pp. 84-87, for description of the American Committee on Foreign Relations.
See also Johnson : "Common Sense in Foreign Policy" (2/6).
Perris : "Our Foreign Policy" (2/6).
Spender : "Foundations of British Policy" (6d.).

## (*b*) INTERNATIONAL LAW.

The difference between the character of International Law and a national code of law should be noted. Compare the agreements and treaties entered into by nations with (i) civil contracts, and (ii) industrial agreements.

Study, in the light of the present state of International Law, (i) England's attack upon Denmark in 1807, and (ii) the violation of the neutrality of Belgium and Luxemburg by Germany in the present war.

Study also the rules relating to the treatment of civilians in occupied territory, contraband of war, etc.

BOOKS : An excellent little manual on international law is Smith : "International Law" (Temple Primers, 1/-). Larger books are Lawrence : "Handbook of International Law" (3/6), and Westlake's "International Law" (4/6.)

For a study of the questions of international law raised in the present war see "Why we are at War," ch. i. and Higgins : " The Law of Nations and the War " (Oxford Pamphlet, 2d.).
Details of the attack by England upon Denmark may be found in any European History. See Fyffe : "History of Modern Europe," ch. vii. (8/-).

## (c) INTERNATIONALISM AND ARBITRATION.

Consider whether internationalism is possible or advisable, and if so, the proper steps to take towards it. Discuss the advantages and difficulties attendant upon compulsory arbitration. Would it be possible for an international Congress to avoid interference with the internal affairs of states ? Would it be safe for a country possessing free institutions to join in an international Congress with nations in which such institutions were absent ? Must not a much greater community of sentiment and outlook prevail among European peoples before the " Parliament of Nations " can be established ?

BOOKS : " War and Democracy " discusses the intimate connection between the growth of democratic sentiment and institutions and the development of Internationalism, chaps. 1 and 9.
Fabian Ware : " The Worker and his Country " (5/-) discusses Internationalism in connection with the Labour movement.
Dasent : " The Story of Burnt Njal " (Everyman, 1 /-) describes the attempt of the hero to substitute communal law for private feud ; see also on this point Zimmern : " Greek Commonwealth" (8/6), part ii, ch. iii.
For a discussion of the principles of International Arbitration see Earl Richards : " International Law and Arbitration " (1 /-), and Hervé : " Internationalism and War " (1 /-).
For details of experiments in internationalism and arbitration (i.e., Hague Conferences, etc.) see Peace Year Book, 1914 (1 /-).

## (d) NATIONALITY : THE PRINCIPLE OF THE COMMONWEALTH.

In the Congress of Vienna the principle of nationality was disregarded, and to this may be traced many of the great wars which have occurred since. This mistake may be repeated in the settlement of the present war, unless the nature of nationality is clearly understood.

What constitutes a nation ? Is a " nation " essential to " nationality " ? Does nationality imply statehood and citizenship ? Must a nation be a sovereign state ? What advantages lie in the preservation of nationality ? While " nationality " and " nation " should not be confused with " state," it will be useful to consider the value of small states such as Servia and Belgium, as against large states such as Great Britain and Austria-Hungary.

Consider the relation of " democracy " regarded as the power of the people to control the destiny of the state to " nationality " ; how far is it true that in the long run the fortunes of " nationality " are bound up with those of " democracy " ?

Books : " War and Democracy," chs. i, ii, and ix, for the discussion of
the whole question.
The principle of nationality.is discussed in Hobhouse : " Social
Evolution and Political Theory " (5/-), pp.146-7, and the same
author, in " Democracy and Reaction " (1 /-), ch. viii, discusses the
connection between the denial of rights of nationality to a
weak people by a strong people, and the decay of democratic
ideas among the latter.
See Powicke : " Bismarck " for the importance of a sense of
nationality in the welding of the German Empire.

## (e) Conceptions of Culture and Civilisation.

The pride of the Germans in their " Kultur " should not
be treated lightly.   Consider the difference between the English
conception of " culture " and the German " kultur." Compare
the Germany of Goethe and Schiller with the Germany of to-day.
Note the difference between cultivation of the character and the
cultivation of the intellect.   Can real culture be imposed upon
a people by the Government ?

Books : " War and Democracy," ch. ix.
Bernhardi : " Germany and the Next War," ch. iv.
Matthew Arnold : " Culture and Anarchy " (6d.).
"Germany in the Nineteenth Century" (Manchester University,
2/6).

## (f) National Service.

It may be argued that the present crisis has proved that if
Britain is to play her part effectively in continental politics she
must have a large army at her disposal.   Study how far this
is desirable ; and, if desirable, how it can be best secured.
Compare the relative merits of (i) relying upon volunteers
being forthcoming in sufficient numbers when the emergency
arises (as in the present case), (ii) a great increase in the
standing army, still secured by voluntary enlistment, (iii) adoption of a system of compulsory training, (iv) adoption of conscription.   In the case of (ii) consider how far the adoption of a much
higher scale of pay, with adequate pensions and provision for
dependents, would secure the necessary recruits.   Study the
provisions for national defence made by continental powers, and
the rates of pay of their soldiers.

The position of non-resistance should be studied, and also
instances of non-resistance (e.g., Penn and his community in
New England, the Doukhobors of Russia, the policy of the Society
of Friends, etc.)

Books : Farrer : " Invasion and Conscription " (1 /-).
Grubb : " True Way of Life " (6d.).
Hamilton, Gen. Sir Ian : " Compulsory Service " (2 /6).
Impey : " Military Training considered as a part of General
Education : National Peace Council Pamphlet (1d.).
Murray : " Peace of the Anglo-Saxons " (2 /6).
Shee : " The Briton's First Duty " (National Service League,
6d.).
Strachey : " New Way of Life " (1 /-).
Earl Roberts : " Fallacies or Facts " (2 /6).
" The Case for Voluntary Service " (King, 1 /-).

UNSECTARIAN    NON-PARTY.    DEMOCRATIC.

# The Workers' Educational Association,

## 14, Red Lion Square, London, W.C.

(Founded August, 1903),

IS A FEDERATION OF OVER

## 2,500 ORGANISATIONS.

It has now :
9 DISTRICT COUNCILS.
180 BRANCHES,
11,430 INDIVIDUAL MEMBERS.

It seeks to fulfil its objects in the following principal ways :—

(A) *By arousing* the interest of the workers in Higher Education, and by directing their attention to the facilities already existing.

(B) *By inquiring* into the needs and feelings of the workers in regard to education, and by representing them to the Board of Education, Universities, Local Education Authorities, and Educational Institutions.

(C) *By providing*, either in conjunction with the aforementioned bodies or otherwise, facilities for studies of interest to the workers which may have been hitherto overlooked.

(D) *By publishing*, or arranging for the publication of, such reports, pamphlets, books, and magazines as it deems necessary.

*Membership is open to Individuals on payment of a Minimum Annual Subscription of 4/-* (including " THE HIGHWAY," post free).
*Affiliation Fee for National and District Organisations, £1 1s. od.*, which entitles a Society to appoint one Representative on the Central or District Council.

---

## LIST OF SECRETARIES.

*General.*—ALBERT MANSBRIDGE, 14, Red Lion Square, London, W.C.
*Assistant.*—DOROTHY W. JONES, 14, Red Lion Square, London, W.C.
*Eastern District.*—G. H. PATEMAN, 117, Lytton Avenue, Letchworth, Herts.
*London District.*—H. GOODMAN, 137, Camberwell Road, S.E.
*Midland District.*—T. W. PRICE, The University, Edmund Street, Birmingham.
*North-Eastern District.*—J. G. TREVENA, 84, Westmorland Road, Newcastle-on-Tyne.
*North-Western District.*—E. J. HOOKWAY, 24, Skakespeare Street, C.-on-M., Manchester.
*South-Eastern District.*—E. W. WIMBLE, 14, Red Lion Square, London, W.C.
*Welsh District.*—JOHN THOMAS, " Penlan," Ebenezer Street, Trecynon, Aberdare.
*Western District.*—W. R. STRAKER, 27, Morgan Street, St. Paul's, Bristol.
*Yorkshire District.*—G. H. THOMPSON, 104, Hyde Park Road, Leeds.
*Women's Department.*—IDA HONY, 14, Red Lion Square, London, W.C.
*Financial.*—E. W. WIMBLE, 14, Red Lion Square, London, W.C.

HON. TREASURER :
JAMES BAMFORD, 14, Red Lion Square, London, W.C.

*Bankers.*—THE NATIONAL AND PROVINCIAL BANK OF ENGLAND, LTD., Aldersgate Street, London, E.C.

The Birmingham Printers, Ltd., 42-44, Hill Street.